Charlie Brown
This Is Your Life

SPARKLER BOOKS
AN IMPRINT OF PHAROS BOOKS • A SCRIPPS HOWARD COMPANY
NEW YORK

Originally published and produced by
Arnoldo Mondadori Editore S.p.A., Milano

Based on the Italian Language Book
''Charlie Brown, tutti i miei ricordi''
(© 1987 United Feature Syndicate, Inc.)
LC 88-042737
ISBN 0-88687-375-4

Printed in Italy

Sparkler Books
An Imprint of Pharos Books
A Scripps Howard Company
200 Park Avenue
New York, NY 10166

10   9   8   7   6   5   4   3   2   1

CONTENTS

Charlie Brown is the focal point of almost every Peanuts story. No matter what happens to any of the other characters, somehow Charlie Brown is involved at the end and usually is the one who brings disaster upon one of his friends or receives the brunt of the blow.
Charlie Brown has to be the one who suffers, because he is a caricature of the average person. Most of us are much more acquainted with losing than we are with winning. Winning is great, but it isn't funny. While one person is a happy winner, there may be a hundred losers using funny stories to console themselves. Just like Charlie Brown.

Charlie on His Own

13

YEARS FROM NOW WHEN I GET DRAFTED, THE ARMY EXAMINER WILL ASK ME WHY I HAVE THIS KITE WITH ME, AND I'LL SAY, "DON'T ASK SUCH STUPID QUESTIONS

At Summer Camp

I HOPE YOU LIKE THIS. POST CARD. PLEASE GREET SALLY FOR ME.

Ladies and Gentlemen, It's Thinking Time

Writer's Cramp

Sports

Little Sister

Charlie and Snoopy

Charlie and Lucy

Charlie and Linus

Patty and the Other Girls

OW!OOO!OW!

OW OWOWOW

THE WORST THING ABOUT SWIMMING IS CROSSING A PARKING LOT! HOT

HOOP HOOP HOOP HOOP